C0-BHG-786

OTHER BOOKS BY GLADYS CONKLIN

I LIKE CATERPILLARS
Pictures by Barbara Latham

I LIKE BUTTERFLIES
Pictures by Barbara Latham

WE LIKE BUGS
Pictures by Artur Marokvia

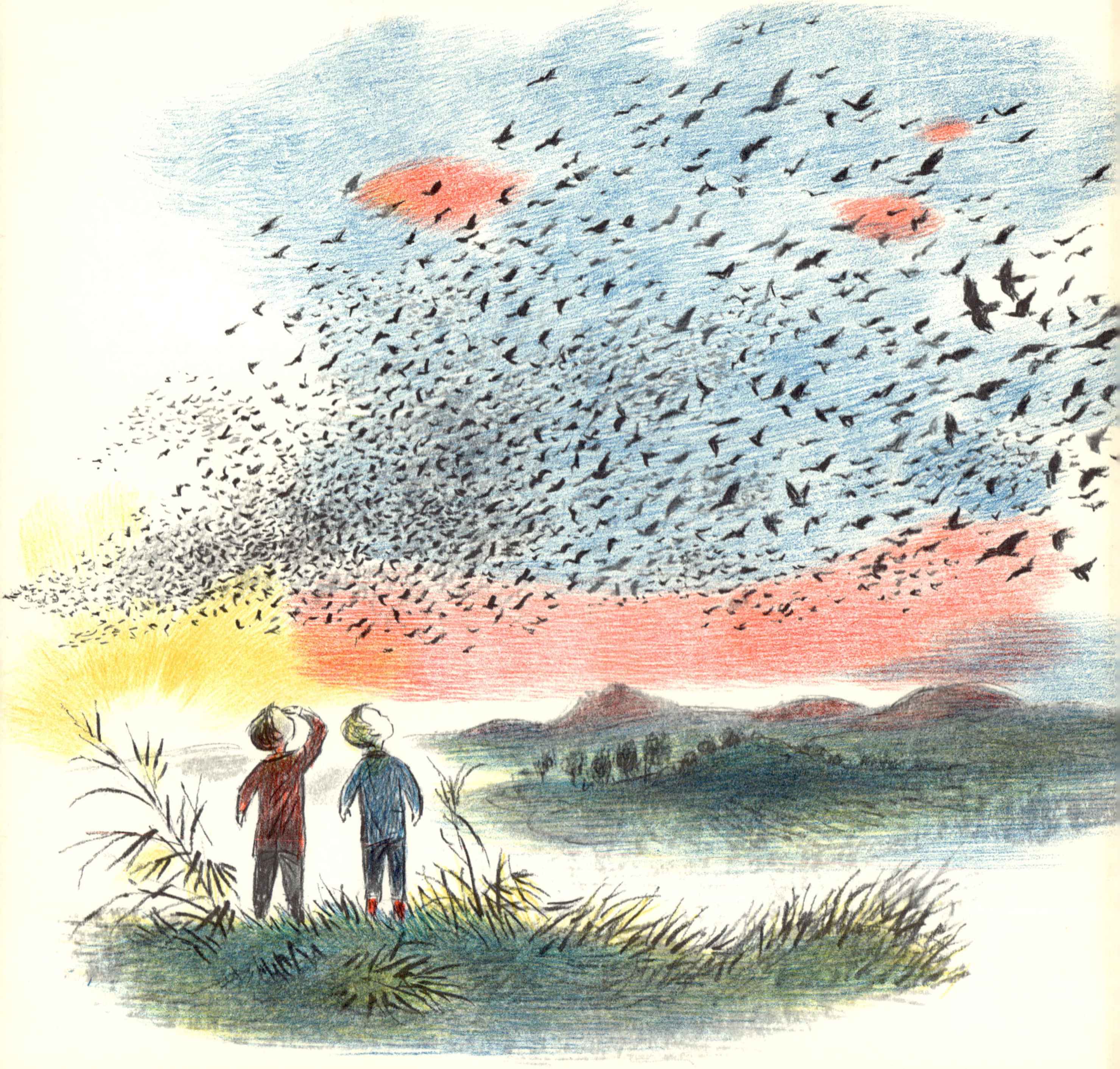

If I Were a Bird

words by Gladys Conklin
pictures by Artur Marokvia

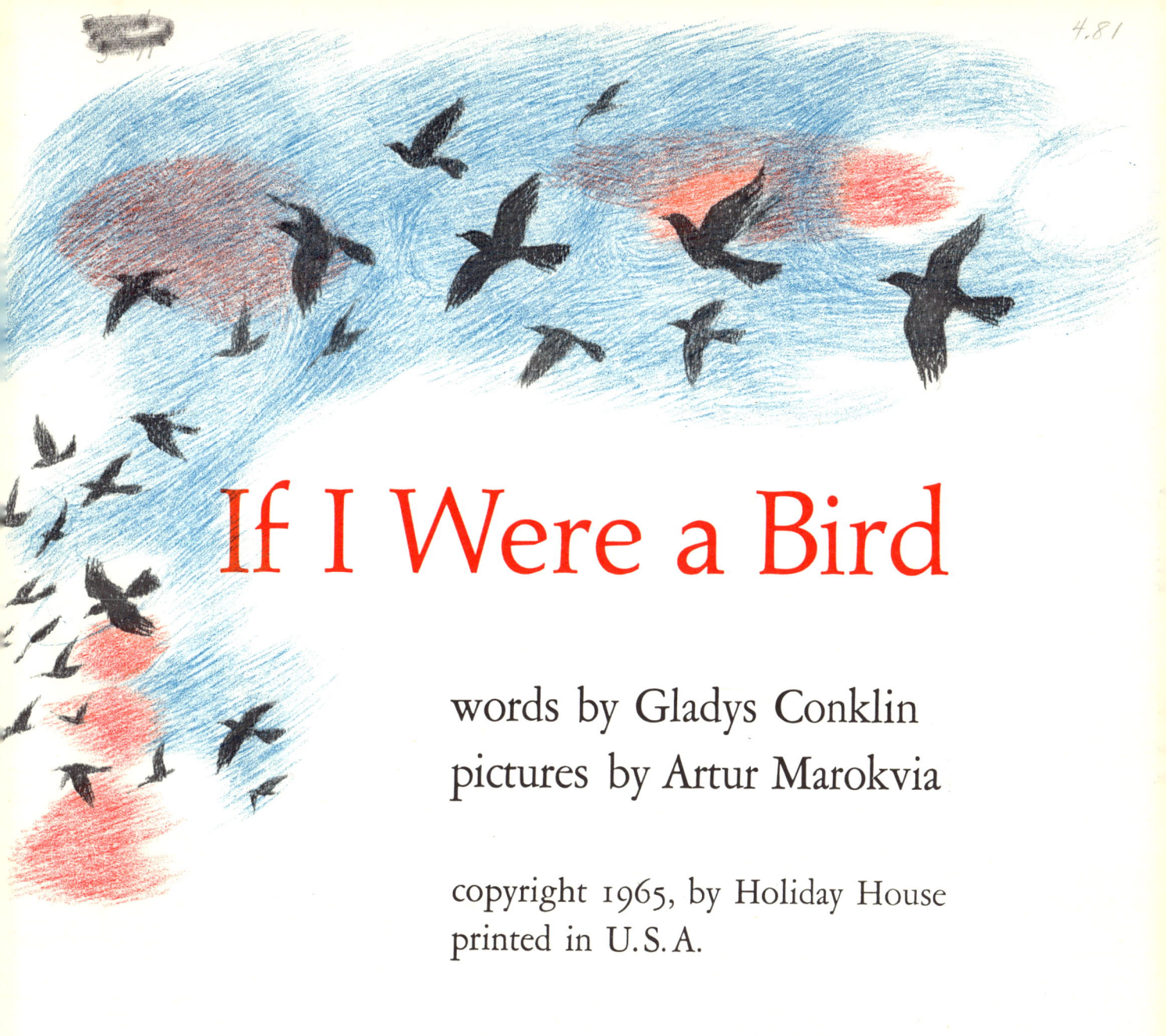

copyright 1965, by Holiday House
printed in U.S.A.

For Frank, Janice, Tad, and Neil
for sharing the blackbirds at sunrise

AUTHOR'S NOTE

This book is to help young children become aware of the pleasures of watching and especially of listening to birds. A bird that cannot be seen can often be heard, and children have the ear to recognize and remember bird calls and songs with ease. The musical notations within the illustrations serve only as clues to each bird's most common, easily recognized song or call. In some instances these are too complicated to be represented in simple note form, and have been omitted. Where musical notations are given, special credit for them goes to the artist, Artur Marokvia, who is also an accomplished musician.

Twenty-seven birds are presented, each one in some typical activity in a place which it frequents. Some birds, such as the kingbird and towhee, vary in coloring, call, etc. in different parts of the country. In such cases I have chosen one of the most familiar, since it was impossible to include them all, and one that I have known and enjoyed.

The feather-collecting pages at the end of the book have grown out of an old hobby, now shared with young friends.

Some records of actual bird songs to use with this book are: *Bird Songs in Your Garden, The Mockingbird Sings,* and *Music and Bird Songs*. These records were made by Cornell University Laboratory of Ornithology, at Ithaca, New York.

—Gladys Conklin

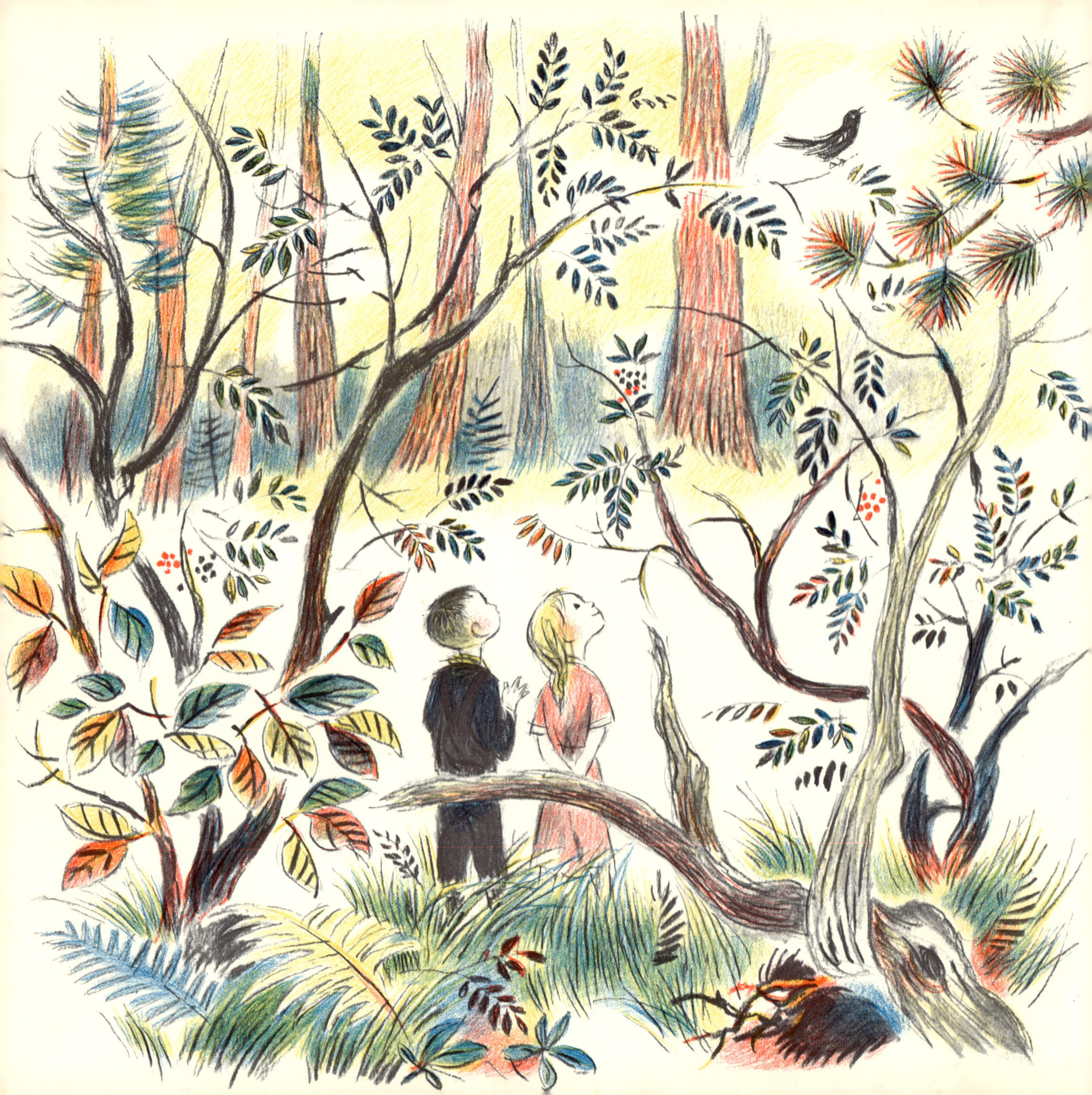

IF I WERE A BIRD,
I could whistle or call or sing
better than I can now.
Feathers would be my clothes, and
I'd keep them smooth and clean.
My arms would be wings,
if I were a bird.
I could fly over a bush
or to the top of a tree
or far through the sky into the clouds.

I listen to the birds
and I watch them.
I'd like to be a bird.
Sometimes I play I am.

If I were a mother grosbeak
I'd build a nest by myself
while my mate sang to me.
He'd be a good father and take turns
sitting on the eggs and
feeding the babies all day long.
They'd open their big mouths and
squawk! squawk! to say, more! more!

In the spring, I'd like to be a tanager
and teach my young ones to fly.
They would cheep–cheep–cheep
when I came near with food.
I'd fly past them and perch and call,
chip–churr–chip–churr!
Then one would follow me, then another.

chip - churr   chip - churr

pee-ik   pee-ik

At dusk, I wish I were
a nighthawk way up in the sky.
I'd fold my wings and dive,
then zoom up so fast
my wings would go B O O M !
If I were a nighthawk
I'd eat mosquitoes and small bugs,
and fly back and forth with
my mouth open to catch them.

When it's time to go to bed,
I want to be a big hooty owl.
I want to float through the air
like a moth, and drop like a rock
to catch a mouse.
Hoo, hoo-oo, hoo, hoo, hoo, I'd call.
My mate would answer,
  hoo, hoo-hoo-hoo, hoo-oo, hoo-oo.

hoo hoo-oo hoo hoo hoo

I wish I were a long-legged killdeer
running through the fields.
When I'd walk I'd bob my head.
If anyone came near my nest
I'd cry and pretend my wing was broken.
Then I'd fly away calling,
kill-dee — kill-dee — kill-dee — kill-dee —

kill-dee   kill-dee

Oo-ah, cooo, cooo, coo!
On warm summer afternoons
I hear this dreamy sound.
It is a mourning dove.
If I were a mourning dove, I'd wear
a feather cape of pink and gray.
With my mate, I'd flutter along
the roadside looking for weed seeds.

oo-ah cooo-cooo-coo

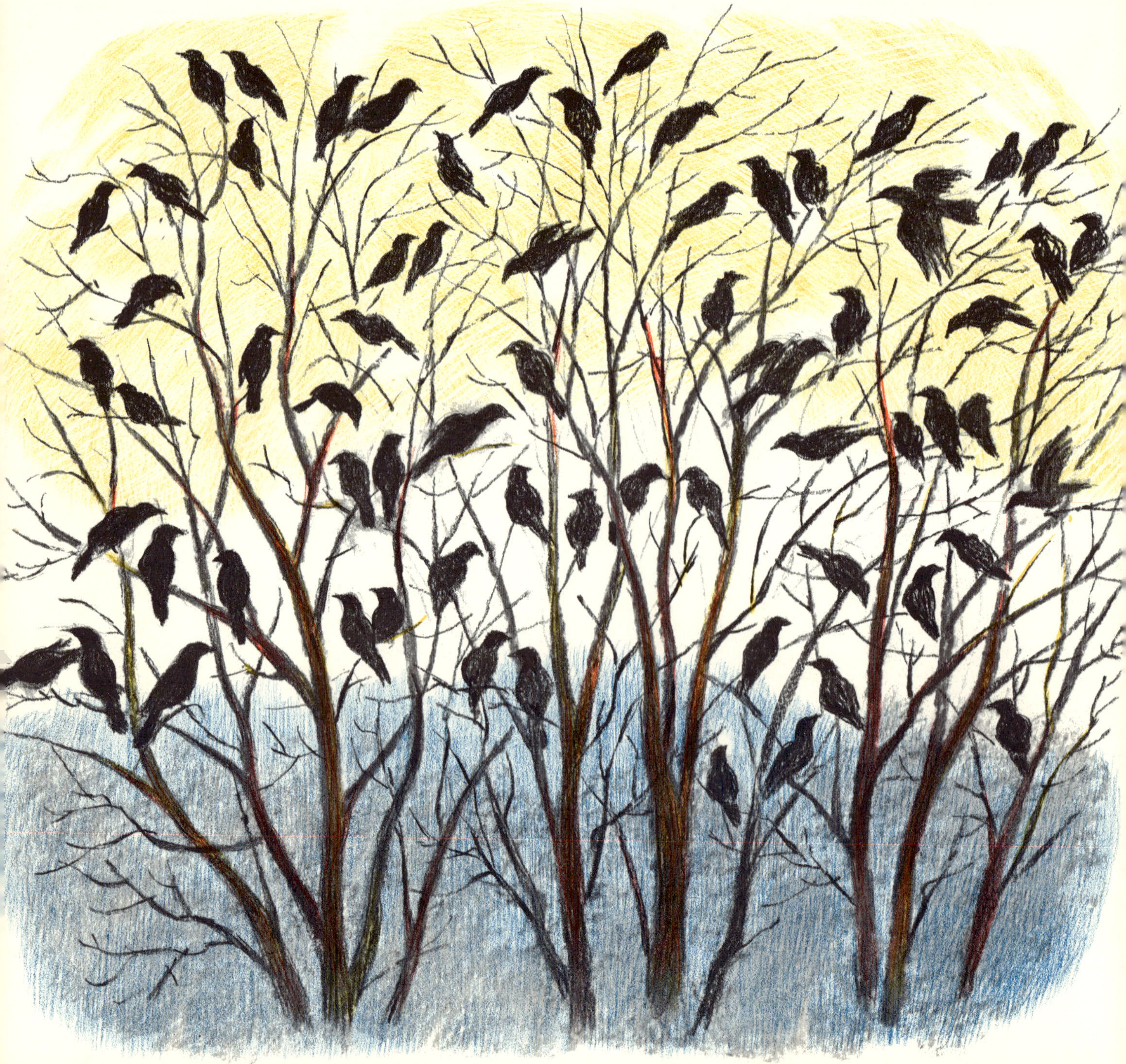

caw ca-a-aw cah cah-ah

When I play I am a crow,
I have many friends.
I live with hundreds of crows.
Our home is a grove of trees.
Before sunup, we all fly away and
hunt and hunt for bugs.
In the afternoon, we come together
and sit and talk.
Caw
    Ca-a-aw, ca-a-aw!
        Cah-ah
           Cah - ah.
              Caw!
At dark, we fly to our roosting trees
and sleep all together —
hundreds and hundreds of us.

wick-wick-wick-etc.....wick

If I were a flicker,
I could call very very fast,
wick-wick-wick-wick,
wick-wick-wick-wick.
Up trees and poles I could walk
with my tail to help me.
Into the wood I could hammer
with my sharp bill.
Bang, bang, bang!
I pull out a beetle.
Bang, bang, bang!
I'd be a drummer if I were a flicker.
I wish I were.

whi whi whi whi whi

If I were a nuthatch,
I could be an upside-down clown.
Down the tree, headfirst,
I could creep.
I'd be hungry for the eggs
in the bark — the eggs
of the bugs that eat the tree.
Eggs for breakfast.
Eggs for lunch.
Eggs for dinner.
Whi, whi, whi, whi, I would whistle.

chewink chewink

If I were a hoppity towhee
I'd call, chewink! chewink! chewink!
I'd hoppity-scratch for beetles
in dry leaves under the bushes.
If you heard me and came to look
I would be still and hide.

che-e-e-er che-e-e-er

When I wake before the sun is up,
I like to think I'm a robin
and sing and sing and sing
a long and beautiful song.
After breakfast I cock my head
and whistle.
In the evening as the sun goes down,
I chirp softly, che-e-e-er — che-e-e-er.

tsee - tsee - tsee ti - ti - ti wee

If I were a warbler,
I'd sit in the top of a tree
and sing to the other birds.
My song would say,
this place is mine-mine-mine!
I'd have dozens of cousins
all in feathers as bright as butterflies —
if I were a warbler.

I'd hang my cradle nest
on the end of a branch,
if I were an oriole.
There my mate would sit and
swing in the wind.
I'd whistle and trill a wild song,
the world was made for me-me-me!

When I feel brave,
I play I am a kingbird.
Dzeeb! dzeeb! dzeeb!
I cry, and chase big birds
away from my tree.
Then I perch and wait for a flying bug.
Out I dart and catch it.

dzeeb dzeeb etc.....dzrrr

When I sing to myself all day,
I am a cheery song sparrow.
I take a bath and splash.
I swish through the garden singing,
sweet-sweet-sweet!
I sing while flying.
I sing while perching.
Over and over and over again,
sweet-sweet-sweet! sweet-sweet-sweet!

I wish I were a red-wing blackbird
swinging on a reed.
I'd spread my wings and sing,
o-ka-leee! o-ka-leee!
Look-at-me! Look-at-me!
My song would warn other birds:
don't build your nest here —
stay away! stay away!

o-ka-leee   o-ka-leee

klee klee klee klee klee

My eyes could see better if I were
a sparrow hawk, high in the air.
Below on the ground I'd see tiny things.
Down I'd go and grab a grasshopper,
or maybe a lizard.
Klee, klee! Klee, klee! I would cry.

chur-wee chur-wee

If I wanted to live in a tree house,
I'd be a bluebird.
My mate and I would bring dry grass
and string for a nest.
We'd try to eat every worm
that dared to show its head.
And I'd sit in the sun and warble.

Some days I play I am
a plain little wren.
I build my nest in a gourd house —
catch a feather, pick up a twig.
I like a clean house.
I gurgle and burble, or
chatter and scold.
And always cock my tail over my back.

When I smell the warm grass,
I am a meadowlark.
I fly low across the grass,
singing as I go.
I flap my wings and sail and sing —
flap and sail and sing.
My voice sounds like a flute.
My song is for rain, for earth, for sun.

When I am a horned lark,
I climb up, up — up to the end of the sky.
My song floats down, down, down,
to the ground —
to my mate at our nest.

In the fall, I'll be a cedar waxwing.
I'll wear smooth, silky feathers
of gray and red and yellow.
I'll travel with a flock of friends,
from place to place, where
we can fill up on fruit and berries.

When I see a flash of green,
I say to myself I'm a tiny hummingbird.
I zip through the air like a small jet
and my wings hum, hum-m-mmm.
Quicker than a wink, I fly backwards.
When I go south for the winter
I can fly five hundred miles.

chick-a-dee-dee-dee

In the cold winter wind,
I'd like to be a chickadee.
I'd fluff out my feathers to keep warm
and swing on a suet bag upside down.
I'd hurry, hurry, here and there.
Chick-a-dee-dee-dee! Chick-a-dee-dee-dee!
    Dee
        dee
            dee!

whoit whoit tu tu tu tu

When the snow is everywhere
I'd like to be a red flashing cardinal
and fight other birds away
from the feeding tray.
Then I'd peck and peck at sunflower seeds.
In the same garden, I'd whistle
and call all winter long.

jeeah   jeeah

On a brisk fall day,
I'd like to be a bold blue jay.
I'd call from the top of a tree,
here! here! here! here!
When enemies came near
I'd dip my head and
jerk my tail and shout,
get out, get out!

What joy! joy! joy! to be a mockingbird.
I'd sing every hour of the day.
I'd sing at night when the moon is full —
call like a robin or chirp like a sparrow,
or sing like other birds I've heard.
When my babies are in the nest,
I'd dive-bomb the cat.
Then zoom to the tallest tree
and sing! sing! sing!

Crow

Horned Lark

Redwing
Blackbird Wing

Sparrow

Towhee

Mockingbird

Hummingbird
Wing

Robin

Flicker

Meadow Lark

Great Horned Owl

Sparrow Hawk

COLLECTING FEATHERS

Spring and summer are the best times to find feathers. It is then that they drop from the birds.

Two feathers drop out at a time, one from each wing. They are really pushed out by new feathers growing underneath. Then the next two drop and two more new ones grow out. The bird changes its tail feathers in the same way: two at a time, one from each side. This keeps the bird in balance and it can still fly. Its body feathers, too, drop and grow one by one.

If a bird lost all feathers at once it would suffer from the cold and wet. It could not fly and might starve.

down feather

contour feathers

flight feather

DOWN FEATHERS are soft and short and grow thick next to the skin.
CONTOUR FEATHERS are longer and grow out over the down feathers. They give a bird its shape and color. Most of the feathers we see when we look at a bird are the contour ones.
FLIGHT FEATHERS are stiff and long and grow on wings and tail.

   The best place to find feathers is wherever you see birds nesting or feeding. You can pick them up in a field, along a road, in woods or a park, or in your own yard or street.

   When you find one, fasten it to a sheet of paper with a bit of Scotch tape. Write the bird's name on the paper. If you do not at first know which kind of bird dropped the feather, fasten it to the paper anyway. Later you may see the same kind of feather on

Grosbeak

Waxwing

Mourning Dove

Yellow Warbler

Blue Jay

a bird or in a picture of a bird. Then you can write the name.

Some birds have different colors of feathers. The males are different from the females, and the young from the parents. Or, the bird will have one color in spring and another color in winter. You can place on each bird's sheet of paper all the different colored feathers you find.

The more feathers you collect, the easier it will be to know which bird dropped them. It will be easy, too, to tell the down feathers and the contour feathers and the flight feathers from one another.

If you find two or three feathers of the same kind you can trade them with friends who are making collections. The feathers will keep for years. The beautiful shapes and colors are a pleasure to look at, again and again.